EDITOR: MARTIN WINDROW

OSPREY MILITARY · **MEN-AT-ARMS SERIES** · **258**

FLAGS OF THE AMERICAN CIVIL WAR 2: UNION

Text by
PHILIP KATCHER
Colour plates by
RICK SCOLLINS

Published in 1993 by
Osprey Publishing Ltd
59 Grosvenor Street, London W1X 9DA
© Copyright 1993 Osprey Publishing Ltd

ISBN 1 85532 255 2

Filmset in Great Britain
Printed through Bookbuilders Ltd, Hong Kong

Author's acknowledgements:
Thanks are due to Ronn Palm, Michael J. McAfee,
Howard Michael Madaus, and Harry Roach.

Artist's Note
Readers may care to note that the original paintings
from which the colour plates in this book were
prepared are available for private sale. All
reproduction copyright whatsoever is retained by the
publisher. All enquiries should be addressed to:
  Richard Scollins
  14 Ladywood Road,
  Ilkeston
  Derbyshire
The publishers regret that they can enter into no
correspondence upon this matter.

Publisher's Note
Readers may wish to study this title in conjunction
with MAA 252 *Flags of the American Civil War (1)
Confederate*.

For a catalogue of all books published by Osprey Military
please write to:

**The Marketing Manager,
Consumer Catalogue Department,
Osprey Publishing Ltd,
Michelin House, 81 Fulham Road,
London SW3 6RB**

INTRODUCTION

The typical flag presentation ceremony of a national colour, here to a Kentucky regiment at Camp Bruce, near Cynthiana, Kentucky.

The regimental or battery set of colours was more than simply a unit designation, issued for the ease of a commander in identifying his units in the field. It was the very symbol of the regiment; it was its heart, the thing that drew its members together. As such it was fiercely defended in action, where it flew in the centre of the line, drawing enemy fire upon its carriers.

Each regiment received its colours in one of its first formal ceremonies, which itself was almost an initiation into the world of the soldier. On 12 November 1861 Pennsylvania's governor Andrew Curtin, accompanied by staff members, took the train from his capital city of Harrisburg to the county seat of Chester County to present a set of colours to the newly formed 97th Pennsylvania Volunteer Infantry Regiment. Arriving shortly after noon, the state officials were met by the entire regiment, which then escorted them to the city's court house. Following a speech introducing the governor and his return

speech to local citizens, the officials had dinner. Then, about three, they all met at the 97th's training camp located on the county fair grounds.

There, according to the regiment's historian: 'The Regiment was formed in column by division closed in mass in front of the stand, on the north side of the Fair buildings. The people had crowded around the reserved space with such eagerness as to render it difficult for the guard to clear sufficient room for the reception committee and those who were to take part in the proceedings.

'When all had been arranged, the Governor came forward, uncovered, holding the staff upon which waved the beautiful stars and stripes of the flag he was about to entrust to the keeping of the regiment, as its banner, around which to rally when led forth into the performance of whatever duty an imperiled country might demand, and, in these words consigned them

3

SIEGE OF CORINTH. MISS. May 1862.

BATTLE OF CHAPLIN HILLS. KY. Oct'r 8th. 1862.

BATTLE OF STONE RIVER. TENN. Dec'31st. 1862.

2nd. BATTALION. 18th. U.S. INFANTRY.

BATTLE OF HOOVER'S GAP.TENN.June 26th.1863. BATTLE OF CHICKAMAUGA.TENN. Sept. 19&20.1863.

SIEGE OF CHATTANOOGA.TENN. Sep'21st.to Nov.23d.1863. BATTLE OF MISSION RIDGE.TENN. Nov.25th.1863.

BATTLE OF RESACCA. GEO. May 14th.1864. BATTLE OF ATLANTA. GEO.

This national colour of the 2d Battalion, 18th US Infantry Regiment has its stars arranged in the canton in the manner of flags made by Evans and Hassall, Philadelphia. (West Point Museum Collection)

to the Regiment. . . .' Curtin spoke at great length, ending with this peroration:

'It is the flag of your fathers and your country. It will be yours to bear it in the thickest of the fight and to defend it to the last. Upon its return, it will have inscribed upon it the record of those battles through which you have carried it, and will become a part of the archives of Pennsylvania; and there it will remain, through all coming time, a witness to your children and your children's children of the valor of their fathers. With a full confidence that in your hands this banner will never be disgraced, I entrust it to your care and for the last time bid you farewell.'

In camp, the regimental colours flew over the unit headquarters as a guide post to members and outsiders alike. In combat, it was drawn into the very centre of action where, in obedience to millions of words like those spoken by Governor Curtin at thousands of presentations, it was fiercely defended. Take, for example, the 38th Pennsylvania Volunteer Infantry Regiment at Antietam. There the regiment

was one of dozens which stormed Confederate positions in the now famous Cornfield. According to the 1865 *History of the Pennsylvania Reserve Corps*, 'A most singular fatality fell upon the color bearers of this regiment. Sergeant Henry W. Blanchard, who had carried the regimental colors through all the storms of battle in which the regiment fought, was a most remarkable man. Born in Massachusetts in 1832, he was about thirty years old. He had the most complete control of his feelings; in the fiercest hours of battle, was always perfectly calm, never shouted, cheered or became enthusiastic, but steadily bore up his flag. At the battle of New Market cross roads, when every color-bearer in the division was either killed or wounded, Sergeant Blanchard received a wound in the arm, he retired a few minutes to have his wound bandaged and then returned to his place. At Antietam he was so severely wounded that the flag fell from his hands, and he was unable to raise it; Walter Beatty, a private, seized the banner to bear it aloft, and almost immediately fell dead, pierced by rebel bullets; another private, Robert Lemmon took the flag from the hands of his fallen comrade, a companion calling out to him, "don't touch it, Bob, or they'll kill you," the brave boy, however, bore up the banner, and in less than a minute lay dead on the ground; the colors were then taken by Edward Doran, a little Irishman, who lying upon his back, held up the flag till the end of the battle, and for his gallantry was made a non-commissioned officer on the field.'

Few things were more disgraceful than losing one's colours in battle, and extreme sacrifices were often made to save them. For example, the 1st Delaware Infantry Regiment were also at Antietam where they were stopped by overwhelming enemy fire, suffering heavy losses. They were driven back, caught between fire from enemy troops in their front and from reinforcements who confused them for Confederates in the fog of battle. Despite tremendous fire, according to the regiment's historian: 'On the ground, a few yards in advance, where the line was first arrested, lay a large number of our men, killed or wounded, and among them lay the colors of the regiment, one of which was held by Lieutenant-Colonel Hopkinson, who was wounded. Major Smyth, Captain Rickards, Lieutenants Postles, Tanner, and Nicholls, Sergeants Dunn and McAllister, with several other non-commissioned officers, rallied a large number of the men for the purpose of returning to the original line, recovering the colors, and holding the position, if possible.

'They sallied gallantly to the front under a terrible tornado of shot, and held the position for a considerable time. . . . When the regiment retired from the field both colors were brought with it, one by Lieutenant C. B. Tanner and the other by Sergeant Allen Tatem, one of the color-guard.'

The generally accepted jargon for the elements of flags and their components is used throughout this book. The *canton* is the square or rectangle placed at the top of the flag next to the pole or staff. A *border* is the flag's edging, when rendered in a colour different from that of the field. The main part of the flag is the *field*. The *hoist* is the side of the flag next to the staff, while the *fly* is the opposite side of the flag. The flag is shown with the hoist on the left and the fly on the right; this is the *obverse* or front of the flag; The side seen when the hoist is on the right and the fly on the left is the *reverse*, or rear. When speaking of measurements, however, flag dimensions are often referred to as being, for example, six feet on the hoist (i.e., along the staff), by five on the fly (i.e., parallel to the ground). The staff itself is the *stave*; the metal object on top of the stave, usually a spearhead, an axehead or an eagle, is the *finial*. The metal cap at the bottom of the stave is the *ferrule*. Many flags have cords and tassels hanging from the finial; collectively, these are simply referred to as *cords*.

Howard Michael Madaus, one of America's leading experts on Civil War flags, holds an authentically reconstructed national colour of the 2d Wisconsin Volunteer Infantry Regiment, which he carried at the 125th anniversary recreation of the battle of First Bull Run. He wears an authentically reconstructed 1861 Wisconsin uniform.

Select Bibliography

Beale, James, *The Battle Flags of the Army of the Potomac at Gettysburg, Penna, July 1st, 2d & 3d, 1863*, Philadelphia, 1885

Billings, John D., *Hardtack and Coffee*, Glendale, New York, 1970

Official, *Atlas to accompany the Official Records...*, Washington, DC, 1891–1895

Madaus, H. Michael, 'McClellan's System of Designating Flags, Spring-Fall, 1862'; *Military Collector & Historian*, Washington, DC, Spring 1965, pp 1–13

Madaus, Howard M., 'The Conservation of Civil War Flags: The Military Historian's Perspective'; *Papers presented at the Pennsylvania Capitol; Preservation Committee Flag Symposium, 1987*, Harrisburg, 1987

Phillips, Stanley S., *Civil War Corps Badges and Other Related Awards, Badges, Medals of the Period*, Lanham, Maryland, 1982

Sauers, Richard A., *Advance The Colors!*, Harrisburg, 1987

Todd, Frederick P., *American Military Equippage*, Vol II, Providence, Rhode Island, 1977

REGULATION FLAGS

The Army of the United States basically had two colours per dismounted regiment, which were issued according to army-wide regulations issued 10 August 1861. From the *Revised Regulations for the Army of the United States, 1861*:

'1436. The garrison flag is the national flag. It is made of bunting, thirty-six feet fly, the twenty feet hoist, in thirteen horizontal stripes of equal breadth, alternately red and white, beginning with the red. In the upper quarter, next to the staff, is the Union, composed of a number of white stars, equal to the number of States, on a blue field, one-third the length of the flag, extending to the lower edge of the fourth red stripe from the top. The storm flag is twenty feet by ten feet; the recruiting flag, nine feet nine inches by four feet four inches.

Colors of Artillery Regiments

'1437. Each regiment of Artillery shall have two silken colors. The first, or the national color, of stars and stripes, as described for the garrison flag. The number and name of the regiment to be embroidered with gold on the centre stripe. The second, or regimental color, to be yellow, of the same dimensions as the first, bearing in the center two cannon crossing, with the letters U.S. above, and the number of regiment below; fringe, yellow. Each color to be six feet six inches fly, and six feet deep on the pike. The

The national colour behind this captain appears to be that of the Governor's Foot Guard, a uniformed but strictly social Connecticut organization. Nonetheless, it shows the eagle finial which often topped the national colour, and the tassels. (David Scheinmann Collection)

The national colour is carried in action in 1861. Note the eagle and streamers.

pike, including the spear and ferrule, to be nine feet ten inches in length. Cords and tassels, red and yellow silk intermixed.

Colors of Infantry Regiments

'1438. Each regiment of Infantry shall have two silken colors. The first, or the national color, of stars and stripes, as described for the garrison flag; the number and name of the regiment to be embroidered with silver on the center stripe. The second, or regimental color, to be blue, with the arms of the United States embroidered in silk on the center. The name of the regiment in a scroll, underneath the eagle. The size of each color to be six feet six inches fly, and six feet deep on the pike. The length of the pike, including the spear and ferrule, to be nine feet ten inches. The fringe yellow; cord and tassels, blue and white silk intermixed.

Camp Colors

'1439. The camp colors are of bunting, eighteen inches square; white for infantry, and red for artillery, with the number of the regiment on them. The pole eight feet long.'

Each foot regiment was to have two camp colours, carried on the extreme right and left of the regiment by sergeants serving as general guides. In fact many of the actual colours violated regulations by having unique insignia on them. The 72nd Pennsylvania Volunteer Infantry, for example, had plain dark blue camp colours with a golden bee painted on a sky blue oval; and the 95th Ohio Volunteer Infantry had scarlet silk camp colours with a golden wreath surrounding the unit designation, '95 OHIO'.

General Orders No. 4, 18 January 1862, said that 'camp colors ... will be made like the United States flag, with stars and stripes'. Surviving camp colours of the 128th New York Infantry were made in this style, with the number 128 on a dark blue cloth field, sewn onto the colour.

The star pattern in the canton of this national colour of the 18th US Infantry Regiment matches those made under a US Quartermaster Department contract by Alexander Brandon, issued through the New York Quartermaster Depot in 1864. (West Point Museum Collections)

Manufacturers' variations

The description of the national flag used as a camp colour, as well as both a garrison and regimental flag in the regulations, was vague in such details as the exact arrangement of the stars in the canton. Indeed, it did not even spell out if the canton were to be square or rectangular. A variety of styles of canton shapes and star designs were seen in actual practice, varying according to the flags' makers.

One basic difference between Army national colours and flags flown by civilians and non-military governmental organizations is that most Army national colours used gold stars while most other American flags had white stars. Apparently this came about when the Army switched to silver embroidery for its stars before the war; silver embroidery thread tarnished to an unsightly black, so gold was substituted for silver—hence the gold stars. Many private manufacturers during the war did embroider white stars on the cantons of the national colours they supplied under state contracts, but Army-issued national colours had gold stars, usually painted rather than embroidered.

Army-issued national colours were provided to regiments which needed replacement colours or did not receive presentation colours from their state government or local organizations. Army-issued colours were issued at the Quartermaster Depots in Philadelphia, New York, and Cincinnati, Ohio. Private contractors between May 1861 and October 1865 supplied the Philadelphia Depot with 890 national colours, the New York Depot with 917 national colours, and the Cincinnati Depot with 500 national colours.

National colours provided by the Philadelphia Depot apparently had the gold stars in their rectangular cantons arranged as a vertical double ellipse with an additional star in each corner. Some had a centre star, while some lacked this final star.

New York Depot national colours had the gold stars in a square canton arranged in five horizontal rows. Until 4 July 1863, when West Virginia was admitted as a new state and a new star was authorized for it, these had six stars in the middle row and seven stars in each of the two outer rows. After 4 July 1863 each row had seven stars. Although Nevada was admitted to the Union on 31 October 1864, no star was authorized to mark that state until after the war was over.

Apparently national colours supplied by the Cincinnati Depot had rectangular cantons with seven horizontal rows of gold stars. Each row except the bottom one had five stars, with four stars in the bottom row until July 1863, when it, too, acquired a fifth.

Most regiments, however, especially early in the war, were presented with national colours by some local group which had acquired them from private contractors. These colours were quite expensive by the standards of the day.

Pennsylvania's state inspector general asked for bids for making flags for the Commonwealth's troops from three local manufacturers. One, Horstmann, asked $160 for a pair of national and regimental colours, $35 for a cavalry standard, and $12 for a cavalry guidon. Evans & Hassall wanted $135 for a pair of national and regimental colours. $35 for a cavalry standard, and $22.50 for a cavalry guidon. Brewer wanted $110 for the infantry colours, $30 for the cavalry standard, and $15 for the guidon. (At this time a private soldier's pay was only $13 a month.)

On 27 November 1861 the adjutant general of Kentucky asked for quotes for making flags for the state's troops from both a local manufacturer, Hugh

Wilkins of Louisville, Kentucky, and Tiffany & Co. of New York City. Wilkins replied: 'I will make infantry regimental colors for $125 per set with the arms of Kentucky on each side of the standard and regular regimental flag stars and stripes with the number of each regiment in gold on each side and the same in the blue flag on a scroll under the coat of arms. Cavalry standards done in a like manner for $45.00 each, guidons for $10.00 each. Artillery flags same as Infantry.'

Tiffany wired: 'Blue regimentals both sides $100.00 each in three weeks, with case, belt, and fringe. National stars and stripes $60.00 each in one week. Guidons embroidered name and number $25.00 pair in two weeks.'

Presentation national colours made by Tiffany went mostly to New York and some Connecticut units, although some were carried by Michigan units and at least one by an Indiana unit. Tiffany colours were embroidered with white stars in a square canton. Until July 1863 they were set in six horizontal rows, the middle two with five stars while the outer two had six stars. Starting in July 1863 the top three rows had six stars each; the fourth row had five; and the bottom two rows had six. Unit designations on Tiffany colours were rendered in script letters.

Presentation national colours made by another New York maker, Paton & Company, used white silk appliquéd stars set in five horizontal rows, the middle one of which had six stars while the upper and lower two had seven stars each, in a square canton. The unit designation appeared in script letters.

Evans & Hassall of Philadelphia, Pennsylvania, arranged the gold stars in the rectangular cantons of their national colours as a simple double ellipse of stars surrounding a single star in the centre, with one gold star at each corner of the canton. New Jersey regiments after 1863 received national colours made by this company.

Horstmann Brothers & Co., a general military equipment and uniform supplier from Philadelphia, also produced presentation national colours for Minnesota troops for a short time starting in late 1862, and for West Virginia's troops after that state's formation. These were made like the Evans & Hassall colours with a double ellipse of gold stars in a rectangular canton. Both Evans & Hassall and Horstmann also produced national colours for Pennsylvania troops, but these differed in that the state seal surrounded by stars was painted in the centre of the canton. The first national colours supplied by Horstmann to New Jersey used this same design, with the New Jersey state seal surrounded by stars in their cantons.

Maryland troops received national colours made by Sisco Bros., of Baltimore, with square cantons and, after July 1863, five horizontal rows of seven gold stars each.

Hugh Wilkins, Louisville, Kentucky, produced national colours for Kentucky troops and, apparently, units from Illinois, Indiana, and Ohio as well. These were unusual in that a light or sky blue was used for the square cantons. The gold stars were arranged in six horizontal rows, five in the top and bottom rows and six in the other rows.

A private of the Veteran Reserve Corps, formed from men no longer capable of active field service but still capable of serving, holds one of the Corps' national colours. (Ronn Palm Collection)

Gilbert Hubbard & Co., Chicago, Illinois, made national colours for units from Wisconsin. Its first ones had the state seal as well as stars in the rectangular cantons. However, replacement colours made until July 1863 had gold stars in six horizontal rows with six in the top, bottom, and two middle rows and five in the second and fifth rows.

Regimental colours were also issued through the three basic quatermaster depots. Between May 1861 and October 1865 the Philadelphia Depot purchased 765 regimental colours; the New York Depot, 1,021 regimental colours; and the Cincinnati Depot, 564 regimental colours.

Many of Philadelphia's regimental colours came from Horstmann and Evans & Hassall. These colours bear the US coat of arms on the eagle's breast over a three-piece red scroll painted with a raised centre section and under a double curve of stars: the top row had 21 stars, the bottom row 13 stars.

New York's Depot had a variety of suppliers including A. Ertle, Paton & Co., and A. Brandon. They had a large, but somewhat unrealistic eagle under two rows of stars, 18 in the top row and 16 in the bottom.

Cincinnati's Depot had several contractors who provided regimental colours of various qualities.

An officer holds a battle-torn national colour bearing three battle honours for engagements in the Army of the Potomac. Note the axehead which tops the stave.

John Shilleto of Cincinnati turned out well-painted eagles with detailed feathers and realistic heads. His first colours had 21 stars in the top row over 13 stars in the bottom, ending at the tail of the motto scroll. His post-July 1863 colours had 20 stars over 15 stars in two rows which extended below the ends of the scroll.

Another Cincinnati supplier, Longly & Bro., turned out eagles which were poorly painted, with ill-defined feathers and a 'black eye' on each eagle's head. Until July 1863 the top row of stars on these flags had 21 stars, over 13 stars in the bottom row; after that date they bore 21 over 14 stars, the latter touching the trails of the motto scroll. The motto scrolls from both makers had lower centre sections.

Hugh Wilkins' regimental colours featured eagles with down-turned heads, as well as another design which had the eagle perched on a US shield in the centre of a circular clouded perch. Both had five-piece red motto scrolls.

Both national and regimental colours, save those presented by local groups and locally made, were issued without regimental designations in the stripe or motto scroll. It was up to each regimental colonel to have the regimental designation put on each colour.

* * *

To return to the 1861 Army Regulations:
'Standards and Guidons of Mounted Regiments
'1440. Each regiment will have a silken standard, and each company a silken guidon. The standard to bear the arms of the United States, embroidered in silk, on a blue ground, with the number and name of the regiment, in a scroll underneath the eagle. The flag of the standard to be two feet five inches wide, and two feet three inches on the lance, and to be edged with yellow silk fringe.
'1441. The flag of the guidon is swallow-tailed, three feet five inches from the lance to the end of the swallow-tail; fifteen inches to the fork of the swallow-tail, and two feet three inches on the lance. To be half red and half white, dividing at the fork, the red above.

A colour-sergeant holding his battle-torn flag. The regiment is unknown. (Ronn Palm Collection)

On the red, the letters U.S. in white; and on the white, the letter of the company in red. The lance of the standards and guidons to be nine feet long, including spear and ferrule.'

Modifications to the 1861 regulations appeared soon after they were published. The first changed the guidons issued to mounted units. According to General Orders No. 4, issued 18 January 1862: '1. Under instructions from the Secretary of War, dated January 7, 1862, guidons and camp colors for the Army will be made like the United States flag, with stars and stripes.'

Mounted units wanted to fly a version of the US national flag. However, not even the modification of January 1862, which gave them a guidon version of the US flag, was enough for many such units; instead, they often flew the whole US flag. Indeed, a message from the commander of the Army of the Ohio, dated 3 June 1862, to Brigadier General Thomas Crittenden noted: 'The general yesterday observed one of the batteries in your division carrying a large flag

COLOR SGT AND BATTLE

FLAG UNKNOWN

11

This national colour used in Virginia in 1861 displays a different star pattern from that usually employed. There were no clear national regulations on the arrangement of stars.

the regular army. But the volunteers seemed to be a law unto themselves, and, while many flags in existence today bear names of battles inscribed by order of the commanding general, there are some with inscriptions of battles which the troops were hardly in hearing of.'

Table A: Unit Designations

Unit designations on national colours were placed on one of the horizontal stripes, often the seventh one from the top. However, this system was far from universal, as seen by the selection of representative national colours which have survived and are listed below. When the stripe is indicated it is counted from the top down. When letters or an abbreviation follow the number or capital letters, such as '2d' or 'REGt', the small letter was usually raised parallel with the top of the larger numbers and one or two dots placed under the small letter.

Unit designation	Designation placement
1st BATn PIONEER BRIGADE	7th stripe
2nd MICH. INF.	7th stripe
2d Wisconsin Infantry Volunteers.	7th stripe
3rd REGt WIS. VETERAN INFANTRY.	7th stripe
7th REGt NEW JERSEY VOLUNTEERS.	7th stripe
13th ILL.	7th stripe
15th REGt Ky VOLs	8th stripe
15th REGt WIS. VOLs.	7th stripe
15th REGt IND. VOLS.	9th stripe
18th Michigan Infantry.	7th stripe
19th REGIMENT/ MASSACHUSETTS VOLs	5th/7th stripes
MASSACHUSETTS VOLUNTEERS/21st. REGT. INFANTRY	4th/6th stripes
28th REG. PENNa VOL. INFy	7th stripe
40th REGt N.J. VOLS.	7th stripe
46th Regt. MASS. MILITIA	7th stripe
46th REGT. O.V.I.	3rd stripe
46th Ohio V.V.I.	Centre of canton
51st REG'T P.V.V.	Top stripe
56th Regiment,/ MASSACHUSETTS VOLs.	5th/7th stripes
60th REG'T O.V.U.S.A.	7th stripe
68th REGT. OHIO VET. VOL. INFANTRY	8th stripe
76th OHIO	7th stripe
154th Regt. NYSV (in script)	7th stripe

instead of a guidon, as ordered. The general desires to know why the orders on this subject are not carried out.'

Battle honours

Shortly after the guidon revision order was issued a practice that had been standard for many years before the war was made official. Regiments and batteries were allowed to indicate their service in battle on their colours. As stated in General Orders No. 19, 22 February 1862: 'It has been ordered that there shall be inscribed upon the colors or guidons of all regiments and batteries in the service of the United States the names of the battle in which they have borne a meritorious part.' The order went on to say that 'It is expected that troops so distinguished will regard their colors as representing the honor of their corps—to be lost only with their lives—and that those not yet entitled to such a distinction will not rest satisfied until they have won it by their discipline and courage.'

This privilege was soon abused by a number of volunteer units which put the names of battles in which they had played the most minor of parts onto their colours. According to John Billings, a veteran of the 10th Massachusetts Artillery, in the Army of the Potomac, 'Originally battles were only inscribed on flags by authority of the secretary of war, that is, in

This was not always the fault of the troops who carried the colours; it was often unclear what unit was authorized what battle honour. Some commanders published lists of battle honours that could be placed on flags, some simply ordered every unit present at any given battle to put the honour on its flag. Even some governors issued orders to their state units to put specific honours on their battle flags.

As a result of this confusion, on 7 March 1865 the Army of the Potomac issued its General Orders No. 10 which listed every volunteer unit in the army along with a list of battles that could be placed on its colours. However, the Army of the Potomac appears to have been the only large organization within the Union forces to attempt to standardize battle honours and, by the time it did so, many of its older units had already been mustered out, their battle flags now hanging in state capital buildings.

* * *

Finally, according to the 1861 regulations: 'The ambulance depot, to which the wounded are carried or directed for immediate treatment, is generally established at the most convenient building nearest the field of battle. A *red flag* marks its place, or the way to it, to the conductors of the ambulances and to

the wounded who can walk.' General hospital flags were in fact yellow, with a large green Roman letter H on the field, and smaller yellow flags with green borders were generally used to mark the way from the firing line to field hospitals. This was standardized by General Orders No. 9, 4 January 1864, which called for a yellow general hospital flag 5 ft. by 9 ft. in size with a Roman letter H, 24 inches tall, on its field. Post and field hospitals had the same flag although only 5 ft. by 9 ft. in size. Rectangular guidons 14 inches by 28 inches edged with one-inch green borders were to mark ambulances as well as the route to field hospitals.

ARMY HEADQUARTERS FLAGS

No special colours were authorized under the regulations for army headquarters. Yet there was a precedent for having a special flag for marking the headquarters of a commanding general; during the War for American Independence, George Washington's headquarters was marked by an all-blue flag bearing 13 five-pointed stars.

In fact, the first flag selected to mark the headquarters of the Army of the Potomac, under General Orders No. 102, 24 March 1862, was a plain national flag. The national flag used by the army's headquarters in 1863, now in the Military Order of the Loyal Legion of the US, Philadelphia, had four rows of seven stars over a last row of six stars in its canton. It was 4 ft. on the hoist by $5\frac{1}{2}$ ft. in the fly. It bears no unit designation or other distinctive marks.

Indeed, veteran John Billings later recalled that 'The stars and stripes were a common flag for army headquarters. It was General Meade's headquarters till Grant came to the Army of the Potomac, who also used it for that purpose.' Therefore, on 2 May 1864

A colour-sergeant of the 141st Pennsylvania Volunteer Infantry Regiment sits in front of the regiment's national and regimental colours. The regimental colour tassel hangs over his right shoulder. (Ronn Palm Collection)

This infantry regimental colour conforms in overall design to those known to have been issued by the New York Quartermaster Depot. The regiment that received it would have been responsible for getting the number filled in properly. (West Point Museum Collections)

the army's final commander, Major-General George G. Meade, adopted a new headquarters flag. According to an army circular issued at that time, 'Hereafter the designating flag for these headquarters will be a magenta-colored swallow tailed flag, with an eagle in gold, surrounded by a silver wreath for an emblem.' Billings said the guidon was actually 'lilac colored'. It measured 4 ft. on the hoist by 6 ft. on the fly (see *MAA 179*, p. 25).

The Army of the Potomac's Artillery Reserve had its own flag, authorized in General Orders No. 119, 30 April 1862. This was a 5 ft. by 6 ft. rectangular red flag with a white star in its centre. This was changed by General Orders No. 53, 12 May 1863, to a red swallow-tailed guidon, of the same dimensions as other corps flags, with a pair of white crossed cannon on its centre. Brigadier-General Henry J. Hunt, Army of the Potomac chief of artillery, apparently adopted a blue guidon with a red Roman letter A surmounting a pair of white crossed cannon for a personal flag in 1864. In October 1864 the Horse Artillery Brigade received a blue triangular flag with red crossed cannon, and the letters H above the cannon and A under them.

Other Army of the Potomac generals flew their own flags. The flag of the chief of engineers, for example, was a blue field, 4 ft. by 6 ft., with a red turreted castle, the symbol of the Corps of Engineers (see *MAA 179*, p. 28).

The Army of the James was created from the X and XVIII Corps in 1864. On 3 May 1864 its headquarters adopted a 6 ft.-square flag divided horizontally into red and blue halves. A large five-pointed star in white was placed in the centre.

When Major-General Philip Sheridan received command of the Army of the Shenandoah he appears to have used a swallow-tailed cavalry guidon to mark his headquarters. The guidon was divided into horizontal halves, the top white and the bottom red. A red five-pointed star was placed on the top half, and a similar star in white on the bottom half. The guidon measured some 3 ft. on the hoist by 6 ft. on the fly.

Under General Orders No. 91, Department of the Cumberland, the flag for department and army headquarters was a national flag 'with a golden eagle below the stars, two feet from tip to tip'. The flag's size was 5 ft. by 6 ft. However, according to General Orders No. 62, 26 April 1864, the headquarters flag was to be a 5 ft.-square national colour; it bore the gold Roman letters 'D.C.' within the canton and a gold eagle clutching a laurel branch in its left claw and five arrows in its right. The motto 'E PLURIBUS UNUM' flew from its beak. The eagle was painted on the field no deeper than the canton. The placement of the eagle is slightly different on the reverse from the obverse.

The Department and the Army of Tennessee and the Army of the Ohio had very similar headquarters flags, both with blue fields and gold fringe, cords and tassels. The Army of Tennessee's flag had the corps badges of the XV and XVII Corps on a vertical background of red, white, and blue. The flag of the Army of the Ohio had the corps badges of the X and XXIII Corps, suspended from sabres, topped by an eagle which looked very much like the colonel's rank badge. It would appear that these two headquarters flags were adopted after they joined the forces under Major-General William T. Sherman in North Carolina in the dying days of the war.

The Military Division of the Mississippi apparently used a 5 ft.-square plain yellow flag as its headquarters flag. In early 1865 the badges adopted by the corps within the division were painted on it.

THE ARMY OF THE POTOMAC

As the Union's field armies grew in size, various of their commanders attempted to make units easy to identify in the field through systems of unique flags carried by each formation and unit. The Army of the Potomac's General Orders No. 102 was issued 24 March 1862, under Major-General George B. McClellan's direction, and gave the Union Army its first comprehensive army-wide flag designating system.

According to the sections which provided instructions on flags, the army's general headquarters would be marked by a plain national flag. Corps headquarters would have a national flag with a small square flag, of a different colour or set of colours, on the same staff under the national flag. The I Corps flag was to be red; II Corps, blue; III Corps, blue and red in vertical halves; and IV Corps, blue and red in horizontal halves.

All divisions had the same size flags, 6 ft. long and 5 ft. wide. The first division of an army corps had a red flag; the second division blue; the third division a vertically divided red and blue flag (contemporary illustrations show that the red half was on the hoist side and the blue on the fly); and the fourth division a horizontally divided red and blue flag.

In fact, however, period writers do not mention any fourth divisions or their flags in the Army of the Potomac for the period. Colonel Charles Wainwright jotted this description in his diary only two days after the new order setting up the flag system was issued: 'One of the first (orders) prescribes the powers of corps commanders, and also designates flags for each headquarters. First Division's [*sic*] will carry a red flag 6 by 5; Second Division's blue; Third Division's red and blue vertical. Ours being the Second will have a blue flag.'

The brigades within each division were marked by different flags, each the same size as the division headquarters flag. Within each first division, the first brigade had a red and white flag in vertical stripes; the second, vertical white, red, and white stripes; and the third, vertical red, white, and red stripes.

The colour guard of the 36th Massachusetts Volunteer Infantry Regiment hold their well-worn colours in this picture dating from late in the war. The two general guides hold their camp colours on either end of the line; these would have flown at either flank of the regiment to mark its position. (US Army Military History Institute)

Within each corps' second division, the first brigade had a vertical striped blue and white flag; the second brigade had vertical white, blue, and white stripes; the third, vertical blue, white, and blue stripes.

The same sized flags were used by brigade headquarters in each corps' third division. The first brigade had vertical red, white, and blue stripes; the second, vertical red, blue, and white stripes; and the third, vertical white, red, and blue stripes.

Among corps with a fourth division, the first brigade had horizontal red, white, and blue stripes; the second, horizontal red, blue, and white stripes; and the third, horizontal white, red, and blue stripes.

Within each brigade, each regiment was to carry in addition to its national and regimental colours a copy of the brigade headquarters flag with the numbers 1, 2, 3 or 4 on it, according to the unit's ranking on the brigade table of organization. White numbers were used on coloured bars and coloured numbers (which often appear to have been red) on white bars. Actual regimental flags measure between 54 and 56 inches on the hoist and between 70 and 72 inches on the fly.

Artillery batteries were to carry the colours of the division to which they belonged as well as a right-angled triangular flag 6 ft. long and 3 ft. wide at the staff. Cavalry units were to have the same as the artillery, although their flag was to be swallow-tailed. Engineer units had a white disc of a diameter equal to one third of its width on the flag of the division to which the unit was assigned.

The Regular Brigade had a white star on a red flag, the regimental number being in the middle of the star. This was changed by General Order No. 119, 30 April 1862, to a 'blue flag with a white star in the center'. In fact, an original flag carried in the brigade is at the Chapel of St. Cornelius the Centurion, Ft. Jay, New York. It is only 18 inches long on the hoist and 3 ft. on the fly, with a white star within an oval green laurel wreath. This flag, carried during the Peninsular Campaign, became the head-quarters flag of the 2d Division, Provisional V Corps, in May 1862 when the brigade was made part of that corps.

Hospitals were distinguished by a yellow flag. As described above, hospital flags were also marked with a Roman letter H in green, and small rectangular guidons of yellow edged with green were used to

A pair of regimental colours in action, 27 June 1862, during the Peninsular Campaign. The national colour is topped with an eagle while the regimental colour has a spike finial. They are both carried in the front and centre of the regimental front.

The regimental colour of the 1st Veteran Reserve Corps Regiment conforms in design to those made by Longly & Bros. under Quartermaster Department contract through the Cincinnati Depot. The 18th Veteran Reserve Corps Regiment regimental colour, however, was made by Horstmann Bros. for the Philadelphia Depot and differs slightly in design. (West Point Museum Collections)

mark the way from the front line to the field hospitals. Subsistence depots were designated by a green flag.

These flags were attached to a portable staff 14 feet long, in two joints, and were supposed to be habitually displayed in front of the headquarters which they designated. On the march they were to be carried near the unit commander.

These orders were modified by General Orders No. 110, 26 March 1862:

'Third Army Corps: National flag with a small square red and blue (instead of blue and red) flag, vertical, beneath.

'Fourth Army Corps: National flag with a small square red and blue (instead of blue and red) flag, horizontal, beneath.'

They were further modified in General Orders No. 119, 30 April 1862, which gave the cavalry reserve headquarters a yellow flag 6 ft. long and 5 ft. wide, with two blue stripes 6 inches in width, crossing

diagonally. The reserve's first brigade had a yellow flag the same size, with one blue star in the centre, while the second brigade had the same flag with two blue stars in the centre. The artillery reserve headquarters received a similar sized red flag with a white star in the centre, while the brigade of regular infantry received a blue flag of the same size with a white star in the centre.

An additional flag was made regulation by General Orders No. 152, 9 August 1862: 'The main (ordnance) depot for the army will be designated by a crimson flag, marked "Ordnance Depot, U.S.A."'

Although the system was all-inclusive, there is some question as to what degree it was actually practised. Regiments tended to get transferred between brigades quite often, meaning that they had to change flags just as often. Moreover, there was bound to be less loyalty to such an arbitrary and abstract flag than to the elaborate regimental and national colours which were distinguished with the unit's actual designation. Even so, there are a number of surviving examples of regimental designating flags, so many must have seen actual use.

On 25 November 1862, after the V Corps was added to the Army of the Potomac, Brigadier-General Daniel Butterfield of that corps wrote to army headquarters: 'In the order designating flags for

The regimental colour bearers for the 111th Pennsylvania Volunteer Infantry Regiment. At the end of the war it was quite popular for units to have their colours photographed so that members could keep the images as mementoes of their service. Note the spearpoint finial on the regimental colour. (Ronn Palm Collection)

A pre-1863 regimental colour for the 5th US Artillery Regiment, with the design smaller in the field than after 1863. (West Point Museum Collections)

Army Corps (orders 102 and 110, Headquarters, Army of the Potomac, March 1862) no flag has been designated for the Fifth Corps.

'I would respectfully request that a flag be designated as shown in the following sketch. For the Fifth Army Corps, viz: Red with a Greek Cross in the center, under the national flag as per General Orders No. 102, Army of the Potomac, and that the Quartermaster's Department be directed to furnish the same.'

Butterfield's sketch did not in fact show a Greek cross, but a cross *botonée*, which is a form of Greek cross save that each arm ends in a trefoil bud.

On 7 February 1863, according to General Orders No. 10, the corps headquarters flags were changed to blue swallow-tailed guidons 6 ft. on the fly by 2 ft. on the hoist, each with a white cross bearing the corps number in red Roman numerals in the centre of the cross. According to the order, the cross was to be a 'Maltese cross', but actual examples show it to have been the cross *botonée* that Butterfield, who designed the corps badges later used in the Army of the Potomac, earlier suggested for the V Corps.

When Major-General Joseph Hooker took over the demoralized Army of the Potomac after the defeat at Fredericksburg and its 'mud march', he began to restore the army's morale. In part he did this through a system of badges unique to each division of each corps, worn on the soldier's hat or coat breast. These unique badges were adapted to a revised system of identification flags carried by divisions and brigades which was made official by General Orders No. 53, dated 12 May 1863.

The cavalry corps headquarters was now to carry a flag of the same size and shape as had been used by infantry corps, but all in yellow with white crossed sabres on its centre. The artillery reserve headquarters flag was to be the same, but in red with white crossed cannon in its centre.

Each division headquarters was to fly a different style flag. Each corps' first division was to have a white rectangular flag with a red corps badge in its centre; the second division had a blue flag with a white corps badge; the third, a white flag with a blue corps badge.

The VI Corps' 'light division' had a white rectangular flag, with a green Greek cross in its centre.

The brigades in each corps' first division had a white triangular flag with a red corps badge in the centre. The first brigade simply carried this colour; the second brigade had an additional 6-inch-wide blue stripe next to the staff; the third, a 4½-inch blue border all around the flag. According to Billings, 'Whenever there was a fourth brigade, it was designated by a triangular block of color in each corner of the flag.'

The brigades of each corps' second division had a blue triangular flag with a white corps badge in the centre. The individual brigade flags used the same system as in the first division, the stripes and borders being red instead of blue.

The brigades of each corps' third division had a white triangular flag with a blue corps badge in the centre. Individual brigade flags used the same system as the first division, the stripe and borders being red.

Although not mentioned in the initial order, soon after it was issued corps artillery headquarters adopted a red brigade flag with the corps badge in white in its centre. The corps quartermaster's headquarters had a blue swallow-tailed guidon the same size as the brigade flags with diagonal white stripes parallel with the swallow tails and ending at the top and bottom of the flag at the staff.

This system of flags to designate specific headquarters in the Army of the Potomac continued in use through the army's existence.

Corps Badges of the Army of the Potomac, 1863

Corps	Badge
I	A sphere
II	A trefoil
III	A lozenge
V	A Maltese cross
VI	A (Greek) cross
IX*	A shield with a figure 9 in the centre, crossed with a fouled anchor and cannon
X*	A four-bastioned fort
XXI*	A crescent, points up
XII*	A five-pointed star

(*Served with the Army of the Potomac at one time or another but was not always a member of that army.)

The IX Corps adopted a fairly complicated badge which did not lend itself to the simple outline style of badge used by the other corps. It involved a cannon crossing a fouled anchor on a shield. Therefore, when the IX Corps adopted its flags to conform with the Army of the Potomac system on 1 August 1864, it called for flags that were slightly more elaborate than those used by the other corps. The headquarters' blue swallow-tailed guidon had a white shield with a red cannon crossing a blue anchor. The first division's blue shield had a blue cannon crossing a white anchor; the second division's white shield had a red cannon crossing a blue anchor; and the third division's blue shield had a white cannon crossing a red anchor.

Towards the end of the war, casualties forced units to be merged, even at corps level. On 26 November 1864 the merger of troops of the remainder of I Corps into Third Division, V Corps resulted in General Orders No. 10 which read in part, 'The Division flag will be the flag now authorized, with a circular belt surrounding the corps, insignia and of the same color.'

On 25 March 1864 the First Division, III Corps became the Third Division, II Corps, and the Second Division, III Corps became the Fourth Division, II Corps. However, Major-General A. A. Humphries, last commander of II Corps, later wrote, 'No power on earth could consolidate or fuse the Third with the Second, and the authorities were at length compelled to let the Old Third wear their Old Third insignia. The men would not discard the Lozenge or Diamond, and Mott's division headquarters flag, The Old Third, bore a white Trefoil on a blue Diamond or Lozenge on its swallow-tail.'

A post-war Quartermaster Department illustration of the regulation artillery regimental colour.

The regimental colour of the 1st US Artillery Regiment fits the style of colours made in 1863 and afterwards. (West Point Museum Collections)

The standard of the 2d US Cavalry Regiment. (West Point Museum Collections)

The Army of the James

The Army of the James was created on 2 April 1864 under Major-General Benjamin F. Butler with the purpose of attacking Richmond from the South. It was created with the X and XVIII Corps, which were discontinued on 3 December 1864 when the XXIV and XXV Corps replaced them.

On 3 May 1864 Army headquarters set up a fairly simple system of flag identification through division level. Headquarters used a 6 ft.-square flag divided horizontally red over blue; a large white five-pointed star was placed centrally on the field. The two colours in the field represented the two corps under its command.

According to an order sent to the X Corps commander on 3 May 1864 from the headquarters of the Department of Virginia and North Carolina: 'By direction of the commanding general of the department, I have the honor to submit the following explanation of the battle-flags to be used by the troops of this command during the coming campaign: The flag carried by department headquarters will be 6 feet square, two horizontal bars, upper bar red, lower bar blue, with a white star in the center; the flag carried by the headquarters Eighteenth Army Corps will be 6 feet square, blood red, with number "18" in the center; First Division flag, same size, blood red, with a single white star in the center; Second Division

flag, same size and color, with two white stars in the center; Third Division flag, same size and color, with three white stars in the center. The flag carried by the Tenth Army Corps will be 6 feet square, dark blue, with the number "10" in the center; First Division flag, same size and color, with a single white star in the center; Second Division flag, same size and color, with two white stars in the center; Third Division, same size and color, with three white stars in the center. Brigade colors will be furnished as soon as practicable.'

This system was abandoned when the XXIV and XXV Corps replaced the original corps in the Army. Both of these corps used Army of the Potomac-style headquarters flags: dark blue swallow-tailed guidons, with a white corps badge and the corps number in red Roman numerals. The XXIV Corps badge was a heart, while that of the XXV Corps was a square. Their division flags were the same as in the Army of the Potomac at that time: white for the first and third divisions, and dark blue for the second division. The corps badge was placed on the field of each, red in the first division, white in the second division, and blue in the third division. Flag sizes in the two corps, however, varied. Division flags in the XXIV Corps were 4 ft. 6 ins. on the hoist by 6 ft. In the XXV Corps they were only 2 ft. 7 ins. by 5 ft. 9 in.

The Department of the Cumberland

On 19 December 1962 General Orders No. 41 was issued by the headquarters XIV Corps and the Department of the Cumberland in Nashville, Tennessee, which divided the forces in the department into 'the center' or 'wings'. Brigades and divisions were assigned into these groups to be numbered from right to left, although referred to by commanders' names in operational reports.

The same order indicated a system of flags to identify the headquarters of these commands:

'III. Flags will be used to indicate the various headquarters, as follows: General headquarters—the National flag, 6 feet by 5, with a golden eagle below the stars, 2 feet from tip to tip. Right wing—a plain light crimson flag. Center—a plain light blue flag. Left wing—a plain pink flag. First Division, right wing—the flag of the wing, with one white star, 18 inches in diameter, the inner point 1 inch from the staff. Second Division, right wing—the flag of the wing, with two white stars, each 18 inches in diameter, the inner points 1 inch from the staff. Third Division, right wing—the flag of the wing, with three white stars, each 18 inches in diameter, set in triangular form, the outside star 1 inch from the outer line of flag. The division flags of the center and left wing will correspond with the above; that is to say, they will be the flags of the center or left wing, as the case may be, and with one, two, or three white stars, each 18 inches in diameter, according as they represent the First, Second, or Third Divisions. The headquarters flags of all brigades will be the flags of their divisions, with the number of the brigade in black, 8 inches long, in the center of each star. That of the brigade of regulars, however, will, instead of the white star and black number, have simply a golden star. The flags of the wings will be 6 feet on staff by 4 feet fly; those of divisions and brigades 5 feet by 3.

They will all be of a pattern to be furnished to the quartermaster's department. Artillery reserve—a plain red flag, equilateral in shape, each side being 5 feet. Cavalry reserve—of the same shape as division flags, 3 feet fly by 5 on the staff, but of deep orange color. Divisions and brigades to be designated as in the infantry; that is, the First, Second, and Third Divisions by one, two, and three white stars respec-

Charging cavalrymen in 1864 carry regulation guidons.

A regulation cavalry guidon carried by an L Troop. (West Point Museum Collections)

tively; the First, Second, and Third Brigades by black figures in each star. Engineer Corps—a white and blue flag, blue uppermost and running horizontally. Flag 5 feet on staff by 3 feet fly. Hospitals and ambulance depots—a light yellow flag, 3 feet square, for the hospitals and for the principal ambulance depot on a field of battle; 2 feet square for the lesser ones. Subsistence depots or store-houses—a plain light green flag, 3 feet square. Quartermaster's depots or store houses—same flag, with the letters Q.M.D. in white, 1 foot long.

'IV. All of these flags will be attached to a portable staff, 14 feet long, made in two joints, and will be habitually displayed in front of the tent, or from some prominent part of the house or vessel occupied by the officer, whose headquarters they are intended to designate; and on the march will be carried near his person.'

This system apparently failed, for General Orders No. 91, issued by the Department of the Cumberland headquarters on 25 April 1863, stated:

'It having been found that the flags prescribed by General Orders, No. 41, from this headquarters, December 19, 1862, to designate the headquarters of the various brigades, divisions, and corps of this army, are not sufficiently marked to be readily distinguished from each other, those herein described will be substituted.

General headquarters The national flag, 6 feet by 5, with a golden eagle below the stars, 2 feet from tip to tip.

Fourteenth Army Corps A bright blue flag, 6 feet by 4, fringed, with black eagle in center, 2 feet from tip to tip, with the number "14" in black on shield, which shall be white.

Twentieth Army Corps A bright red flag, same as that for Fourteenth Army Corps, except the number on the shield, which shall be that of the corps.

Twenty-first Army Corps A bright red, white, and blue flag (horizontal), same as that for Fourteenth Corps, except the number on the shield, which shall be that of the corps.

First Division, Fourteenth Army Corps The flag of the corps, except the eagle and fringe, with one black star, 18 inches in diameter, point 2 inches from staff.

Second Division, Fourteenth Army Corps The flag of the corps, except eagle and fringe, with two black stars, each 18 inches in diameter, inner point 2 inches from staff.

Third Division, Fourteenth Army Corps The flag of the corps, except eagle and fringe, with three black stars, each 18 inches in diameter, set equally along staff, the inner point being 2 inches from staff.

Fourth Division, Fourteenth Army Corps The flag of the corps, except eagle and fringe, with four black stars, each 18 inches in diameter, three of them along

This regulation cavalry guidon was carried by the Cleveland Guards, officially known as L Troop, 1st Rhode Island Cavalry Regiment. (North Carolina Museum of History)

The 1864 headquarters flag of the Department of the Cumberland measures 4 by 4½ ft. The painted eagle is gold, as are the letters 'D.C.' (West Point Museum Collections)

staff as before, the other set equally on the flag.

Fifth Division, Fourteenth Army Corps The flag of the corps, except eagle and fringe, with five black stars, each 18 inches in diameter, three of them along the staff, the other two equally distributed on flag.

The division flags of the Twentieth and Twenty-first Army Corps will correspond with the above, that is, the corps flags (without eagle and fringe), with one, two, three, &c., stars, according as they represent the first, second, third, &c., divisions.

The headquarters flags of all brigades will be the flags of their divisions, with the number of the brigade in white, 8 inches long, in center of each star.

The Regular brigade will have the corps and division flag, but the stars shall be golden instead of black.

Artillery reserve Two bright red flags, each 4 feet by 2, one above the other.

Batteries Each battery shall have a small flag, corps colors, and arrangement (but 1 foot 6 inches on staff, by 2 feet fly), with the letters and numbers of the battery inscribed thereon in black, 4 inches long, thus, "B, First Ohio."

Cavalry headquarters A bright red, white, and blue flag, 6 feet by 4, colors running vertically, red outermost.

First Cavalry Division A bright red, white, and blue flag, 6 feet by 4, like last, with one star, 18 inches in diameter, black, the point 2 inches from staff.

Second Cavalry Division Same as last, except two black stars, each 18 inches in diameter.

'As for infantry, the headquarters flags of brigades will be the flags of divisions, with the number of the brigade in black, 8 inches long.

Engineer Corps A white and blue flag, blue uppermost, and running horizontally, 6 feet by 4.

Hospitals and ambulance depots A light yellow flag, 3 feet by 3, for hospitals and the principal ambulance depot on the field of battle, 2 feet square for the lesser ones.

Subsistence depots and storehouses A plain light green flag, 3 feet square.

Quartermaster's depots or storehouses Same flag, with letters Q.M.D. in white, 1 foot long.

Ordnance department, general headquarters A bright

green flag, 3 feet square, with two crossed cannon in white, set diagonally in a square of 3 feet, with a circular ribbon of 6 inches wide and 3 feet greatest diameter (or diameter of inner circle 2 feet), with the letters "U.S. Ordnance Department," in black, 4 inches long, on ribbon, and a streamer above flag, 1 foot on staff by 4 feet long, crimson color, with words "Chief of Ordnance" in black, 6 inches long.
Division ordnance Same flag, with cannon and ribbon, but no streamer.'

The XIX Corps

The XIX Corps included all the troops stationed in the Department of the Gulf between 5 January 1863 and 20 March 1865. On 18 February 1863 Department headquarters issued General Orders No. 17 which designated unique flags within the Corps:

'III. The various headquarters of the Department of the Gulf will be designated by small flags or guidons, 4 feet square, attached to a lance 12 feet long, made in two joints, as follows:

William McIlvaine, a soldier in the Army of the Potomac, sketched the headquarters of General Andrew Humphreys, 3d Division, V Corps, near Falmouth, Virginia on 30 March 1863. The identifying flag made regulation by General McClellan is on the smaller flagpole. It is halved red and blue, the red towards the hoist and the blue towards the fly. (National Archives)

1: National Colour, 3d US Inf. Regt.

2: National Colour, 1st Bn., 11th US Inf. Regt.
3: Regimental Colour, 6th US Inf. Regt.

A

1: Regimental Colour: 164th NY Inf. Regt.
2: Standard, 2d US Cav. Regt.
3: Regimental Colour, 5th US Arty. Regt.
4: Regimental Colour, artillery

1

2

3

4

B

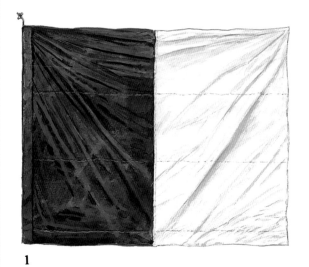

1

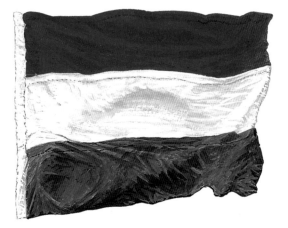

3

2

4

Designating flags, Army of the Potomac
1: 1st Bde., 2d Div. of a Corps
2: 3d Bde., 1st Div. of a Corps
3: 1st Bde., 4th Div. of a Corps
4: 11th Penn. Volunteer Inf. Regt.

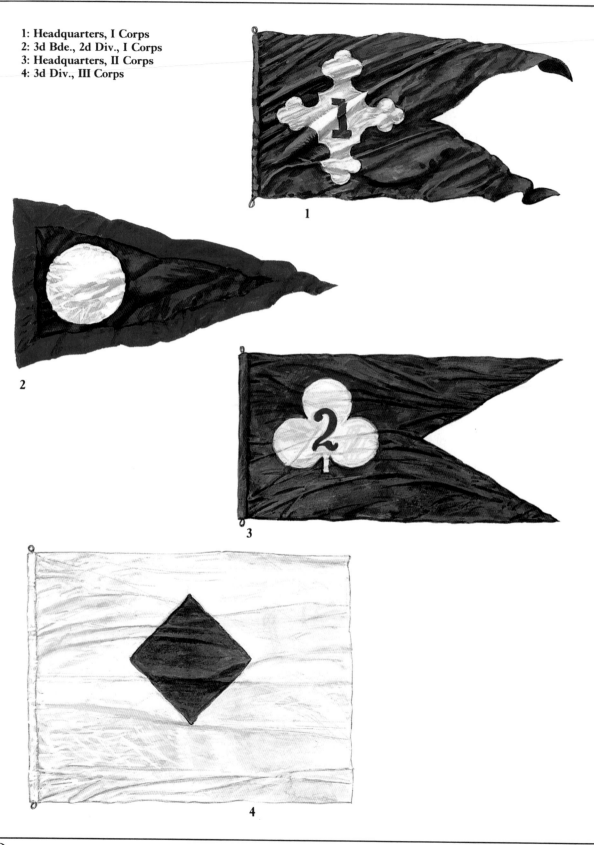

1: Headquarters, I Corps
2: 3d Bde., 2d Div., I Corps
3: Headquarters, II Corps
4: 3d Div., III Corps

D

1: 2d Div., V Corps
2: 1st Div., VI Corps
3: Headquarters, IX Corps
4: Headquarters, X Corps

E

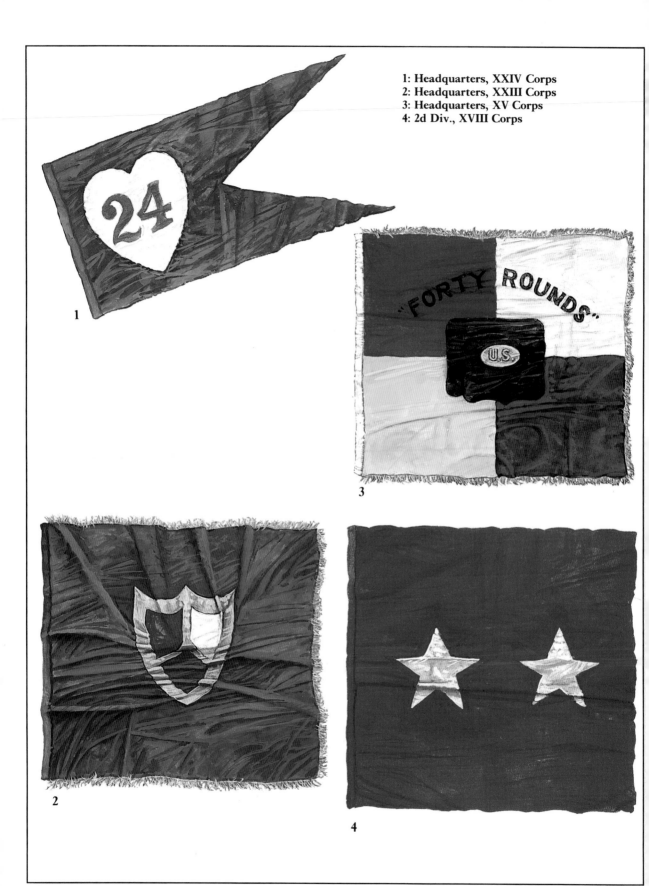

1: Headquarters, XXIV Corps
2: Headquarters, XXIII Corps
3: Headquarters, XV Corps
4: 2d Div., XVIII Corps

F

1: 2d Div., XIX Corps
2: Headquarters, XX Corps
3: Headquarters, IV Corps
4: 3d Div., IV Corps

G

1: Co., I, 6th Penn. Cavalry
2: Headquarters, XXI Corps
3: Headquarters, Cavalry Corps, Army of the Potomac

H

This elaborate flag marks the headquarters of the 2d Brigade, 4th Division, IX Corps, and dates from 1864. Its stripes are, from hoist, green, blue, and red, with a red number '2' and a white shield. The anchor is blue and the cannon red. It measures $2\frac{1}{2}$ by 4 ft. (West Point Museum Collections)

'The headquarters of the Nineteenth Army Corps and the Department of the Gulf by a flag, with a white four-pointed star in the center; the figure 19, in red, in the star.

'Division headquarters, red, with a white four-pointed star in the center; the number of the division in black figures in the star.

'Brigade headquarters, blue, white and horizontal stripes of equal width, the number of the brigade in black figures in the white stripes.'

General Orders No. 11, dated 17 November 1864, indicated both the corps badge and a unique set of flags for the XIX Corps:

'The flags will be as follows: For the headquarters of the corps, blue swallow-tail, seventy-two inches in length by thirty-nine on staff, with white cross eighteen inches square. For the headquarters of divisions, triangular, sixty-six inches in length by forty-four in staff, with cross fifteen inches square. First Division, red, with white cross; Second Division, blue, with white cross; Third Division, white, with blue cross. For the headquarters of brigade, rectangular, thirty-six inches in length by thirty on staff with cross fifteen inches square. First Brigade, First Division, blue and white, horizontal (blue underneath), red cross; Second Brigade, First Division, blue and red, horizontal (blue underneath), with cross; Third Brigade, First Division, red and white, horizontal (red underneath), blue cross; First

Brigade, Second Division, blue and white, perpendicular (blue on staff), red cross; Second Brigade, Second Division, blue and red, perpendicular (blue on staff), white cross; Third Brigade, Second Division, red and white, perpendicular (red on staff), blue cross; Fourth Brigade, Second Division, blue and red, perpendicular (red on staff), white cross; First Brigade, Third Division, blue and white, diagonal (blue on staff), red cross; Second Brigade, Third Division, blue and red, diagonal (blue on staff), white cross; Third Brigade, Third Division, red and white, diagonal (red on staff), blue cross.'

The XXIII Corps

The XXIII Corps, created 27 April 1863 from troops in Kentucky in the Department of Ohio, also served in the Department of North Carolina until disbanded 1 August 1865. Special Field Orders No. 121, 25 September 1864, stated that:

'The badge of the Twenty-third Corps is an escutcheon in the form of the heraldic shield, all of whose proportions are determined by the width, as follows: The sides of the shield are straight from the top for the distance of one-fourth the width of the shield. Each curved side is struck with the center at the lower point of the straight part of the opposite side and with a radius equal to the width ...

'The flags of the corps are as follows: For corps headquarters, a blue flag with a shield in the center of

Although this Army of the Potomac headquarters flag would appear to be that of the 2d Division, I Corps, with a white disc on a blue field, there is no explanation for it being in the headquarters of Brigadier-General Samuel W. Crawford, who commanded the 3d Division, V Corps when this photograph was taken in 1864. The old I Corps merged into the 2d and 4th Divisions, V Corps, in March 1864. (US Army Military History Institute)

the form prescribed; the body of the shield divided into three panels, one panel at each principal angle of the shield; the upper left-hand panel red, the upper right-hand panel white, the lower panel blue, the whole surrounded by a gold outline one-twelfth as wide as the shield. For headquarters Second Division, the whole of the interior of the shield white, otherwise the same as the corps flag. For headquarters Third Division, the whole of the interior of the shield blue, otherwise the same as the corps flag. For brigade headquarters, a flag similar to the division flag, but with smaller shields along the inner margin

corresponding in number to the brigade. The artillery will wear the badge of the division to which the different batteries are respectively attached.'

According to one of its members, Major-General Jacob D. Cox, writing in 1887, the system of corps-wide flags lasted throughout the corps' existence. 'The *Corps Headquarters* flag was a silk banner of dark Army blue color, with gold fringe, and the corps badge emblazoned in the center. The Division Headquarters flags were, *1st Division*, Blue silk banner, yellow worsted fringe, the shield with the same shape as the corps shield in outline & panels, but the panels red in the gold outline. *2d Division*, Similar to the last with all the panels white. *3d Division*, Similar to last, with all the panels blue. The 3d Div. flag shows only the gold frame of the shield, the panels being of the same blue silk as the flag.

'The *Brigade Headquarters* flags were of blue bunting without any fringe. They were of the same

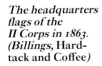

The headquarters flags of the II Corps in 1863. (Billings, Hard-tack and Coffee)

CHIEF Q'R. MASTER.   CORPS H'DQ'RS.   ARTILLERY BRIGADE.

1ST DIV.   2ND DIV.   3RD DIV.

1ST BRIGADE.   1ST BRIGADE.   1ST BRIGADE.

2ND BRIGADE.   2ND BRIGADE.   2ND BRIGADE

3RD BRIGADE.   3RD BRIGADE.   3RD BRIGADE.

4TH BRIGADE.

SECOND CORPS FLAGS 1863

style of shield as the division flags, but the shield smaller, & instead of being placed in the center of the flag, as many shields used indicated the number of the brigade, and they were placed in the corner of the flag where the Union Jack [*sic*] is in the National flag: Shields: 1st Div. Yellow frame, red panels; 2d Div. Yellow frame, white panels; 3d Div. Yellow frame, blue panels. The yellow frame of the shields on the brigade flags was usually made by tenacious yellow paint, the panels being of the red, white, or blue bunting, inserted in the blue flag.'

Third Division, Department of West Virginia

According to General Orders No. 7, issued 23 March 1864 by the headquarters, Third Division, Department of West Virginia: 'I. Hereafter flags will be used to designate the different headquarters of this division, as follows.

'For the division: A three-striped red, white, and blue flag—the stripes to be of width, running diagonally from top to bottom—red at top and white in center, five feet on the staff and six feet fly. The division to be designated by three blue stars thirteen inches long on the white field, the inner corner of which to be five and one-half inches from the staff.

'The brigade flags will be the same as that of the division, with the number of the Brigade in white, six inches long, in the center of each star. These flags to be attached to portable staffs twelve feet long, in two joints, and in the field will be displayed at the quarters of the officers whose headquarters it is intended to designate, and on the march, will be carried near that person.'

Major-General Winfield Scott Hancock, wearing a hat and with one hand on the tree, stands in front of the headquarters flags of the II Corps, the blue swallow-tail flag and a smaller national colour. (US Army Military History Institute)

CAVALRY FLAGS

Originally, Union forces divided cavalry units up among corps, which were largely infantry with artillery support. However, combat soon taught them that cavalry was best used independently; and each army soon adopted cavalry corps, marked by their own flags.

According to General Orders No. 119, 30 April 1862, in the Army of the Potomac, the Cavalry Reserve headquarters was to have a yellow rectangular flag with a blue St. Andrew's cross; the 1st Brigade, a blue star; and the 2d Brigade, two stars. General Orders No. 53, 12 May 1863, gave a yellow swallow-tailed guidon with white crossed sabres to the Cavalry Corps headquarters. Its formations used

This 1864 drawing shows two III Corps headquarters flags, that of the corps headquarters and the white flag with either a red lozenge for the 1st Division or a blue lozenge for the 3d Division.

guidons of their own design, although most were made in the regulation horizontally halved form, red over white, with the division number in the opposite colour on each bar. Other units divided their guidons into three triangles—white on the hoist, blue on the top, and red on the bottom. A pair of crossed sabres was applied to the white triangle, while gold stars were often painted in the other two.

On 1 August 1864 a full system of Army of the Potomac Cavalry Corps colours was approved. It was very smilar to those used by the Army's other corps, with crossed sabres substituted for the corps badges,

Battle honours were often placed on headquarters flags as well as unit flags, although this was not strictly according to orders. This photograph of Major-General David B. Birney, who commanded the 1st Division, III Corps (bottom, centre, with two medals on his chest) shows both the corps headquarters flag and the division headquarters flag. The latter has battle honours, one for Chancellorsville to the right of the lozenge, painted on it in scrolls. (US Army Military History Institute)

complete with a dark blue swallow-tailed guidon for the corps headquarters, white and blue rectangular flags for the division headquarters, and pointed guidons for brigades.

On 26 April 1864 General Orders No. 62, Department of the Cumberland, prescribed a system of flags for its cavalry corps. The corps headquarters had a red, white, and blue flag similar to the French tricolour, with a large pair of gold crossed sabres

extending over all three bars, and fringed in gold. The first and third divisions had white rectangular flags, the first with red crossed sabres and a blue number 1, the third with blue crossed sabres and a red number 3. The second division had a blue flag with white crossed sabres and a red number 2. Brigades received guidons generally following the Army of the Potomac corps flag system.

General Orders No. 3, 24 March 1864, in the Cavalry Corps, Military Division of the Mississippi, produced a different system of flags for that corps' seven divisions. All of its formations had swallow-tail guidons, that for the headquarters being red with yellow crossed sabres, while the divisions had white guidons with dark blue crossed sabres and the division number in red both above and below the sabres.

NAVAL FLAGS

Each commissioned ship of the US Navy and US Marine Revenue Cutter Service flew several flags. A jack, which was simply the dark blue canton with its white stars of the National Flag, was flown at the jack staff of the vessel's bow. A National Flag was flown from different staffs, according to the type of vessel; and a commission pennant identified the ship as a vessel of war. This was a long narrow flag, of blue with a line of white stars at the hoist, and two stripes, red above white.

Captains in command of squadrons, and later admirals, were entitled to fly (or 'wear' as it was then termed) a plain blue flag with as many white stars as there were states. In the case of several squadrons merging, the senior officer would use the blue flag while the next in rank had a red flag. If there was a third captain commanding a squadron in the group, he was entitled to fly the same flag in white.

In February 1865 the admiral's flag was changed from square to rectangular.

A contemporary illustration of the V Corps headquarters flag and one of its division headquarters flags. The headquarters flag marked with the backwards 'C' is probably intended to have a '6' for the VI Corps.

THE PLATES

A1: National Colour, 3d US Infantry Regiment, 1861
The national colour carried by the country's oldest continuously serving infantry regiment, the 3d, was made under federal contract through the Philadelphia Depot. It displays one of three known patterns of stars in its canton. The lower star is missing from the lower ring in the 34-star variety, while the 35-star variety has no central star but has 21 stars in the outer ring.

A2: National Colour, 1st Battalion, 11th US Infantry Regiment, 1863
This is a Tiffany & Company, New York, presentation national colour with typical script-embroidered

Brigadier-General Charles Griffin (standing with open coat and slouch hat) commanded the I Division, V Corps, in late 1863 when this photograph was taken. The headquarters flag is white with a red Maltese cross. (US Army Military History Institute)

unit designation and battle honours. According to tradition, this colour was presented on 22 February 1862; the battle honour for Gettysburg (1–3 July 1863) would indicate that this is incorrect. Apparently the 11th through 19th US Infantry Regiments, which had three battalions, issued regimental colours for their first two battalions, which usually served apart (although probably also to their third battalions, which served as depots if, as few were, they were even organized).

A3: Regimental Colour, 6th US Infantry Regiment, 1863

The 6th Infantry's regimental colour was a Cincinnati Depot federal contract model, believed made by John Shilleto of that city. He received orders for five infantry regimental, two artillery regimental and five national colours on 3 November 1862. Some varieties of these flags have different numbers of stars, yet all have an upper arc that overlaps the end of the motto scroll.

B1: Regimental Colour, 164th New York Infantry Regiment, 1864

This flag was supplied under a New York Depot federal contract. Similar colours display 34 stars; these have only 16 stars in the lower arc.

B2: Standard, 2d US Cavalry Regiment, 1861

Cavalry standards were smaller than those carried by foot regiments for two reasons: there was not as much need for unit identification of mounted units on the field as for foot units; and, the larger the flag, the more difficult it was to carry on the march or in action.

B3: Regimental Colour, 5th US Artillery Regiment, 1862

Cords and tassels on artillery colours were red and yellow intermixed silk, and crossed cannon replaced the national eagle shown on infantry colours. The colours were also the same size for both infantry and artillery regiments.

B4: Regimental Colour, artillery, 1864

In 1863 the design on the artillery regimental colour was enlarged to fill more of the field. This particular colour was made under a New York Depot federal contract. Often partially decorated scrolls were placed on a colour issued to a regiment, which would then be responsible for having the number filled in. This was true of infantry as well as artillery colours.

C1: Designating flag, 1st Brigade, 2d Division of a Corps; Army of the Potomac, 1862

Under the 1862 system of designating flags issued in the Army of the Potomac, each first brigade of a second division, regardless of corps, was to carry this blue and white flag, which measured 5 ft. by 6 ft. This actual flag is in the collection of the US Army Military Academy Museum, West Point, New York. It measures 58 inches at the hoist by 72 inches in the fly.

C2: Designating flag, 3d Brigade, 1st Division of a Corps, Army of the Potomac, 1862

This is another surviving example of an 1862 Army of the Potomac designating flag. This one, which measures 60 inches by 72 inches, is in the New York State Collection.

C3: Designating flag, 1st Brigade, 4th Division of a Corps; Army of the Potomac, 1862

This designating flag, now in the West Point collection, was probably carried in Ord's Division of the Department of the Rappahannock. It measures 54 inches by 70 inches.

This sketch shows the 1st Division, V Corps headquarters flag being carried into battle at Preble's Farm, Virginia, on 30 September 1864.

This photograph of X Corps commander Major-General Alfred H. Terry (in the coat with two rows of buttons arranged in threes) shows the standard Army of the Potomac corps headquarters flag being used in that corps instead of the rectangular blue flag bearing a plain number 10 as ordered in the Army of the James. (National Archives)

C4: Designating flag, 11th Pennsylvania Volunteer Infantry Regiment, 1862

The colours and number on this flag indicate that the unit that carried it was the fourth regiment of the third brigade of the second division, of the III Corps of the Army of the Potomac. In this case, the regiment was the 11th Pennsylvania, which carried this flag in the Second Battle of Manassas.

D1: Headquarters, I Corps, 1863

On 7 February 1863, under General Orders No. 10, all corps headquarters in the Army of the Potomac were to have blue swallow-tailed guidons with a white 'Maltese cross' bearing the corps number in red. This odd device, which is not a true Maltese cross by any means, became the standard symbol used. It is actually a cross *botonée*, that is a Greek cross with a trefoil bud at the end of each arm.

D2: 3d Brigade, 2d Division, I Corps, 1863

The Army of the Potomac system of identifying flags adopted on 7 February 1863 gave corps headquarters a swallow-tailed guidon, with a rectangular flag carried by each division headquarters, and this type of guidon by each brigade headquarters. The white circle is the I Corps badge, which was also worn on soldiers' and officers' headgear and, at times, on the left breast. On 1 August 1864 the corps badge was authorized by General Orders No. 115 to be used on all corps flags.

D3: Headquarters, II Corps, 1864

On 1 August 1864, General Orders No. 115 changed the II Corps headquarters flag by using the assigned Corps badge, a 'trefoil', in place of the 'Maltese cross'. The same device appeared on all this corps' flags, in red for the first division, white for the second division, and blue for the third division. The artillery brigade had a red guidon with a white trefoil, while the corps chief quartermaster had a dark blue swallow-tail guidon with a St. Andrew's cross in white.

D4: 3d Division, III Corps, 1864

Under the system of 1 August 1864, all 3d Division, III Corps flags used a blue corps badge, the lozenge; the 1st and 3d Divisions' headquarters had white flags (with a red lozenge for the 1st Division), whilst the 2d Division headquarters had a blue flag with a white lozenge. The brigade guidons matched the colours, with the first brigade having plain white, the second having a red stripe at the hoist, the third being bordered in red, and the fourth with red tips. Actually III Corps had been merged into II Corps by the time these flags were ordered, although many did see use until the system was changed by Special Orders No. 320, issued 24 November 1864. The flag of the 3d Division under those orders, now in the New Jersey State Capital, has a white background with a blue trefoil within a red lozenge on the field.

E1: 2d Division, V Corps, 1864

The corps badge of the Army of the Potomac's V Corps was the Maltese cross, which appears in white on its 2d Division's headquarters flag. The V Corps received elements of the old I Corps as the V Corps' 2d and 4th Divisions on 24 March 1864. The old I Corps units were allowed to keep their old corps badges and unit flags; on 11 September 1864 all the I Corps elements were further reduced to the 3d Division, V Corps, complete with their old insignia. On 20 December 1864 a circular ordered all men of the division to wear a 'White Maltese Cross' on their hats and all elements of the old I Corps badges were done away with.

E2: 1st Division, VI Corps, 1864

Although originally the Greek cross worn by the VI Corps was ordered to be worn 'upright', it appeared as a St. Andrew's cross on a number of headquarters flags carried within the Corps starting in 1864. The Greek cross was carried in the 3d Division; the other divisions used the St. Andrew's cross.

E3: Headquarters, IX Corps, 1864

The IX Corps adopted this unusual corps badge,

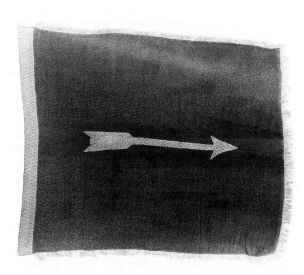

This headquarters flag, in blue with a red arrow and yellow fringe, measures $3\frac{1}{2}$ by $4\frac{1}{2}$ ft., and identified the 1st Division, XVII Corps in 1865. (West Point Museum Collections)

signifying its service as a landing force along the south-eastern coast, on 10 April 1864. The first Corps headquarters flag used the Army of the Potomac's 'Maltese cross' design with a red number 9; it was replaced by a national flag with a corps badge in the canton, surrounded by an oval of stars, in April 1864. This flag was adopted when the Corps was attached to the Army of the Potomac in May 1864, although one source says it was not adopted until 1 August 1864. The divisional flags were red (1st Division), white (2d Division), blue (3d Division), and green (4th Division) with a corps badge of a facing colour. Rectangular brigade flags had three vertical stripes with a corps badge and brigade number.

E4: Headquarters, X Corps, 1864

On 3 May 1864 the X Corps adopted square flags for its headquarters and division headquarters. While the number 10 was used on the corps headquarters flags, the divisions had one, two, and three white stars respectively on their blue flags. On 22 May 1864 the Corps' commander wrote: 'I have received four flags. I propose to replace the stars on the division flags by the corps badge, which is a square bastioned fort, very like a star in effect, I presume there can be no objection to this.' There has been no reply found and, moreover, photographs show the older flag with number 10 in use until the corps' demise in December 1864. Photographs of the recreated corps headquarters, taken after March 1865, show the Army of the Potomac's blue swallowtail guidon with white 'Maltese cross' and red number 10 being used.

F1: Headquarters, XXIV Corps, 1865

The corps badge of the XXIV Corps, Department of Virginia, created from elements of the old X and XVIII Corps, was adopted on 1 March 1865. It consisted of the corps number in red within a white

(Left) *The flag carried by the Chief Quartermaster, XIX Corps, in 1864–65 featured a red cross on a white disc on a blue field. It measures 2½ by 3½ ft. (West Point Museum Collections)*

(Right) *The headquarters flag of Brigadier-General Hugh Judson Kilpatrick (standing behind seated lady), who commanded cavalry in the Army of the Cumberland, had red and white stripes, with a white disc in the centre around an eagle mounted on a national colour in natural colours. The word 'TUEBOR' was painted in black. The photograph was taken in Stevensburg, Virginia, in March 1864 (US Army Military History Institute)*

There are some flags which were clearly made for unit identification but whose purpose is unknown today. This flag, for example, was found among the effects of Thomas Low of Tennessee, who served in the 2d US Tennessee Infantry, which was in the 7th Division in Alabama at one point. It appears to be some sort of identification flag for that unit, but no orders establishing its design have been found. It has a white field, with red stripes along the fly, and blue four-pointed stars, a blue eagle, and blue number 7. (Mike Miner Collection)

heart. The flag measures 36 inches at the hoist by 72 inches in the fly.

F2: Headquarters, XXIII Corps, 1864

Special Field Orders No. 121, dated 25 September 1864, of the XXIII Corps, Army of the Ohio, read: 'The flags of this corps are as follows: For corps headquarters, a blue flag with a shield in the corner of the form prescribed; the body of the shield divided into three panels, one panel at each principal angle of the shield; the upper left-hand panel red, the upper right-hand panel white, the lower panel blue, the whole surrounded by a golden outline one-twelfth as wide as the shield. For headquarters Second Division, the whole of the interior of the shield white, otherwise the same as the corps flag. For headquarters Third Division, the whole of the interior blue, otherwise the same as the corps flag. For brigade headquarters, a flag similar to the division flag, but with smaller shield along the inner margin corres-

ponding in number to the brigade. The artillery will wear the badge of the division to which the different batteries are respectively attached.' The 1st Division presumably received the same flag with a red shield on joining the corps in the spring of 1865.

F3: Headquarters, XV Corps, 1865

By General Orders No. 21, dated 9 April 1865, the XV Corps adopted its corps badge of a cartridge box under the motto 'FORTY ROUNDS' as the centre-piece of its flags. The rectangular flags carried by headquarters and division headquarters were 5 ft. by 5 ft. 6 ins. The division flags were all red for the 1st Division, white for the 2d, blue for the 3d, and yellow for the 4th; the corps headquarters flag was quartered in the three first division colours. Swallow-tailed guidons were carried by brigade headquarters. These measured 4 ft. by 5 ft. 6 ins. and came in appropriate division colours with different borders to designate the different brigades. The corps badges on surviving examples have been painted on the fields.

Major-General David M. Gregg (seated, wearing a slouch hat) commanded the 2d Division, Cavalry Corps, Army of the Potomac. The red and white division

headquarters flag is tied to his tent pole. (US Army Military History Institute)

F4: 2d Division, XVIII Corps, 1864

The XVIII Corps, of the Army of the James, first adopted the same type of flags as used in the X Corps, with the corps number in white on the headquarters flag, and one, two, or three stars, according to the division, on each division headquarters flag. Instead of the blue fields of the X Corps, the XVIII Corps used red. However, on 7 June 1864 a 'cross with foliate sides', similar to the 'Maltese cross' used on Army of the Potomac corps headquarters flags, was adopted as the corps badge. A new corps headquar-

ters flag using this device appears to have been taken into use around July 1864.

G1: 2d Division, XIX Corps, 1864

On 18 February 1863, XIX Corps, of the Department of the Gulf, issued its General Orders No. 17 which called for a headquarters flag: 'A blue flag with a white four-pointed star, in the center; the number 19, in red, on the star.' Each division flag was 'red, with a white four-pointed star, in the center, the number of the division in black figures on the star'. General Orders No. 11, 17 November 1864, revised the system to use the corps' newly adopted badge, 'a fan-leaved cross with octagonal center'. Headquarters used a blue swallow-tailed guidon with a white corps badge, while the guidon used by the 2d Division reversed the colours.

G2: Headquarters, XX Corps, 1864

The XX Corps of the Army of the Cumberland was formed on 4 April 1864 from units of the XXII Corps and the XXI Corps. On 26 April Department of the Cumberland General Orders No. 62 awarded its headquarters a blue swallow-tailed guidon with a white 'Tunic cross' and the red number 20. Old XXII Corps flags were used by the division headquarters, with a 6 ft. square white flag with a blue star in the 3d Division, and a red field with a green star in the 4th Division. Triangular flags, each side being 6 ft. long, were used by brigade headquarters; these followed the Army of the Potomac system for differentiating brigades.

G3: Headquarters, IV Corps, Army of the Cumberland, 1864

The IV Corps of the Army of the Cumberland was different from most corps in that its badge, an equilateral triangle, was not used in any form on the corps flags. Instead, corps and division headquarters used red flags with a blue canton. Headquarters used a golden eagle in its canton.

G4: 3d Division, IV Corps, 1864

Each division of the IV Corps used white stripes to make a design in the blue cantons of their otherwise red flags. The 1st Division had one stripe running diagonally from bottom left to top right; the 2d had a white St. Andrew's cross; and the 3d, a white St. Andrew's cross with a vertical stripe through the middle. Brigades had swallow-tailed guidons with the same canton as their division, but with one, two, or three white stars under the canton according to the brigade number.

H1: Co. I, 6th Pennsylvania Cavalry (Rush's Lancers), 1863

This regulation cavalry guidon was carried by the cavalry company that accompanied the headquarters of the Army of the Potomac during the Battle of Gettysburg. The battle honour for that engagement would therefore suggest that it was carried for some time at least after July 1863. The cavalryman holding the guidon wears the dress jacket worn by mounted troops, trimmed in yellow for cavalry.

H2: Headquarters, XXI Corps, 1863

The oddly-shaped XXI Corps flags were prescribed in the Department of the Cumberland's General Orders No. 91, 25 April 1863. The corps headquarters flag, which was 6 ft. in hoist by 4 ft. in the fly, used an eagle with the number 21, while divisions had from one to three stars on the white stripe. Brigades used the division flags, but with the white number of the brigade replacing the star.

H3: Headquarters, Cavalry Corps, Army of the Potomac, 1864

Cavalry in the Army of the Potomac used a variety of systems of flag identification, starting from 1862 when a blue St. Andrew's cross on a yellow field was authorized for the cavalry reserve headquarters. On 12 May 1863 it was authorized a yellow swallow-tailed flag with white crossed sabres in the centre. Thereafter most cavalry commands used crossed sabres, the traditional Cavalry Corps badge, on their flags. This headquarters flag was adopted in 1864 and apparently used until the end of the war.

Notes sur les planches en couleur

A1 Ce drapeau national était porté par le régiment d'infanterie du pays qui avait servi depuis le plus longtemps sans interruption: le 3ème. Il présente un de trois arrangements connus d'étoiles dans son canton. A2 Voici un drapeau national présenté par Tiffany & Company, New York, avec le nom de l'unité et les honneurs des batailles typiquement brodés en lettres manuscrites. A3 Certaines variations de ce drapeau ont différents nombres d'étoiles, mais ils ont tous un arc supérieur qui dépasse la fin du listel de la devise.

B1 Ce drapeau a été fourni dans le cadre d'un contrat fédéral avec le New York Depot. Des drepeaux similaires ont 34 étoiles; ceux-ci n'ont que 16 étoiles dans l'arc inférieur. B2 Les étendards de cavalerie étaient plus petits que les étendards d'infanterie car de grands drapeaux étaient difficiles à porter durant la marche ou pendant l'action, et il était moins nécessaire d'indentifier les unités. B3 Les fanions avaient la même taille pour les régiments d'infanterie et d'artillerie, mais les cordons et pompons des fanions de l'artillerie étaient rouges et jaunes et un cannon croisé remplaçait l'aigle national. B4 En 1863 le dessin sur le fanion du régiment de l'artillerie a été agrandi pour remplir plus de place sur la table d'attente. Souvent des listels partiellement décorés étaient placés sur le fanion, le régiment étant responsable de l'apparition du numéro.

Farbtafeln

A1 Diese Nationalfahne wurde vom 3. Infanterieregiment getragen, dem ältesten in kontinuierlichem Einsatz befindlichen Regiment des Landes. In ihrem Feld zeigt sie eine der drei bekannten Anordnungen der Sterne. A2 Das ist eine von Tiffany & Company in New York gestiftete Nationalfahne mit typischen gestickten schriftlichen Kennzeichnungen und Auszeichnungen. A3 Manche Varianten dieser Fahne haben eine verschiedene Anzahl von Sternen, aber alle zeigen einen oberen Bogen über dem Ende des Motto-Schnörkels.

B1 Diese Fahne wurde unter einem föderativen Kontrakt des New York-Depots geliefert. Ähnliche Fahnen zeigen 34 Sterne; diese haben nur 16 im unteren Bogen. B2 Kavallerie-Standarten waren kleiner als die der Infanterie, weil sie dadurch leichter beim Ritt oder auch im Gefecht zu tragen waren, und weniger Bedarf nach Regimentsidentifizierung bestand. B3 Bei Infanterie- und Artillerieregimentern waren die Fahnen gleich groß, doch waren die Schnüre und Quasten der Artillerieregimentfahne rot und gelb, und sie zeigten gekreuzte Kanonen anstatt des Adlers. B4 1863 wurde das Design auf der Artillerie-Regimentfahne vergrößert, um mehr von dem Feld auszufüllen, und es wurde dem Regiment überlassen, die eigene Nummer hinzuzufügen.

C1 Selon le système de 1862 qui désignait les drapeaux devant être émis à l'Armée du Potomac, chaque première brigade d'une seconde division, sans égard au corps, devait porter ce drapeau bleu et blanc, qui mesurait 5 pieds par 6 pieds. C2 Un autre exemple survivant d'un drapeau de désignation de 1862 de l'Armée du Potomac, mesurant 60 pouces par 72 pouces. C3 Ce drapeau de désignation était probablement porté par la division Ord du Département du Rappahannock. Il mesure 54 pouces par 70 pouces. C4 Les couleurs et chiffres indiquent que l'unité qui portait ce drapeau était le quatrième régiment de la troisième brigade de la seconde division, un Corps III de l'Armée du Potomac.

D1 Le 7 février 1863, tous les sièges des corps de l'Armée du Potomac ont reçu l'ordre d'avoir des guidons bleus à deux pointes avec une croix de Malte, le numéro du corps étant en rouge. Cette croix grecque tréflée avec un bouton de trèfle au bout de chaque bras est le symbole qui a en fait été utilisé. D2 Ce drapeau de quartier général de brigade adopté le 7 février 1863 a un cercle blanc avec le badge du corps. D3 Le 1er août 1864, les Ordres Généraux no. 115 ont changé le badge du quartier général de quartier général assigné, une trèfle, à la place de la croix de Malte. D4 Selon le système de 1864, tous les drapeaux de 3ème division du Corps III utilisaient un badge de corps bleu, le lozange, sur un fond blanc.

E1 Le badge de corps du Corps V de l'Armée du Potomac était la croix de Malte, qui apparaît en blanc sur son drapeau de quartier général de 2ème division. E2 Bien qu'à l'origine la croix grecque portée par le Corps VI devait être portée droite, elle apparaît droite sur un certain nombre de drapeaux de quartier général à partir de 1864. E3 Le IXème Corps adopta ce badge de corps inhabituel, signifiant son service en tant que force de débarquement le long de la côte du sud-est le 10 avril 1864. E4 Le 3 mai 1864, le Xème Corps adopta des drapeaux carrés pour ses quartiers généraux et ses quartiers généraux de division. Le numéro 10 était utilisé sur les drapeaux des quartiers généraux du corps.

F1 Le badge de corps du XXIVème Corps, Département de Virginie, créé à partir d'éléments du vieux Corps X et XVIII, fut adopté le 1er mars 1865. F2 Les Ordres Spéciaux de Terrain No. 121, datés du 25 septembre 1864, du XXIIIème Corps, Armée de l'Ohio, ont créé ce drapeau. F3 Ce drapeau de quartier générale de corps est divisé en quartiers selon ses fanions divisionnels et mesure 5 pieds par 5 pieds 6 pouces. F4 Le 7 juin 1864 le XVIIIème Corps, armée du James, adopta une croix à côtés foliés comme badge de corps.

G1 Le XIXème Corps, Département du Golfe, adopta ce nouveau badge de corps, 'une croix palmée avec centre hexagonal', le 17 novembre 1864, remplaçant l'étoile à quatre pointes. G2 Formé le 4 avril 1864, le XXème Corps de l'Armée du Cumberland a reçu son drapeau de quartier général le 26 avril, un guidon bleu a deux pointes avec une croix tunicelle blanche et un numéro 20 rouge. G3 Notez l'aigle doré dans le canton. A la différence de la plupart des badges de corps du Corps IV, un triangle équilatéral ne fut pas utilisé sous quelque forme que ce soit sur le badge de corps. G4 Chaque division du Corps IV utilisa des rayures blanches pour faire un motif dans les cantons bleus de leurs drapeaux rouges pour le reste. Dans ce cas, une croix de St André blanche avec une rayure verticale au milieu.

H1 Ce guidon de cavalerie de règle était porté par la société de cavalerie qui accompagnait les quartiers généraux de l'Armée du Potomac durant la bataille de Gettysburg. H2 Les drapeaux du XXIème Corps ont des formes bizarres à côté des fanions des autres troupes, ayant 6 pieds de haut et 4 pieds de large. H3 Après 1863, la plupart des commandes de cavalerie utilisaient des sabres croisés, le badge du Corps de Cavalerie traditionnel, sur leurs drapeaux. Ce drapeau de quartier général fut adopté en 1864 et apparemment utilisé jusqu'à la fin de la guerre.

C1 Unter dem Designationssytem von 1862 für Fahnen der Armee am Potomac erhielt jede erste Brigade einer zweiten Division ungeachtet des Korps diese blaußweiße Fahne in den Abmessungen 152 × 182. C3 Diese Designationsfahne wurde wahrscheinlich in der Ord's Division des Departments von Rappahannock getregen – 137 × 177cm. Farben und Zahlen lassen erkennen, daß diese Fahne vom 4. Regiment der 3. Brigade der 2. Division des III. Korps der Potomac-Armee getragen wurde.

D1 Am 7. Februar 1863 wurden alle Korps-Hauptquartiere angewiesen, blaue Schwalbenschwanz-Wimpel mit einem weißen Malteserkreuz und einer roten Korps-Nummer zu tragen; es handelte sich dabei in Wahrheit um ein griechisches Kreuz botoneé mit einer kleeblattförmigen Knospe am Ende eines jeden Arms, und es wurde dann zum Standard-Symbol. D2 Diese Brigaden-Stabsfahne, angenommen am 7. Februar 1863, zeigt einen weißen Kreis mit dem Korps-Abzeichen. D3 Durch den Allgemeinen Befehl No. 115 vom 1. August 1864 wurde das Abzeichen der II. Korps verändert – mit einem Kleeblatt anstelle des Malteserkreuzes. D4 Unter dem System von 1864 zeigten alle Fahnen der 3. Division des III. Korps ein blaues Korps-Abzeichen, die Raute, auf Weißem Grund.

E1 Das Korps-Abzeichen des V.Korps der Potomac-Armee war das Malteserkreuz, hier in Weiß auf dieser Stabsfahne der 2. Division. E2 Obwohl das Griechische Kreuz des VI. Korps urspünglich aufrecht getragen werden mußte, erscheint es ab 1864 auf verschiedenen Stabsfahnen als Andreaskreuz. E3 Das IX. Korps nahm dieses ungewöhnliche Abzeichen an als Hinweis auf seinen Einsatz als Landetruppe entlang der Südostküste am 10. April 1964. E4 Am 3. Mai 1864 nahm das X. Korps rechteckige Stabs- und Divisionsfahnen an. Die Zahl 10 wurde auf den Stabsfahnen getragen.

F1 Das Abzeichen des XXIV. Korps, Department of Virginia, entstanden aus Elementen der alten Korps X und XVIII, wurde am 1. März 1865 angenommen. F2 Diese Fahne wurde durch Spezialbefehl No. 121 vom 25. September 1864 angenommen. F3 Diese Korps-Stabsfahne ist in die Divisionsfarben geviertelt und mißt 152 × 167cm. F4 Am 7. Juni 1864 nahm das XVIII. Korps, Army of the James, ein Kreuz mit Laubwerkverzierungen als Abzeichen an.

G1 Das XIX. Korps, Department of the Gulf, nahm am 17. November 1864 dieses neue Abzeichen an, ein "fächerblättriges Kreuz mit achteckigem Zentrum", anstelle des bisherigen weißen, vierspitzigen Sterns. G2 Das am 4. April 1864 gebildete XX. Korps der Army of the Cumberland erhielt am 26. April seine Stabsfahne, ein blauer Schwalbenschwanz-Wimpel mit einem weißen Kreuz und der Nummer in Rot. G3 Goldener Adler im Feld. Im Gegensatz zu den meisten anderen Korps wurde das Abzeichen des IV. Korps, ein gleichseitiges Dreieck, nie auf den Korpsfahnen getragen. G4 Jede Division des IV. Korps benutzte weiße Streifen, um in den blauen Feldern seiner ansonsten roten Fahnen ein Design zu formen – in diesem Falle ein weißes Andreaskreuz mit einem vertikalen Streifen durch die Mitte.

H1 Dieser vorschriftsmäßige Kavallerie-Wimpel wurde von der Kompanie getragen, die das Hauptquartier der Potomac-Armee während der Schlacht von Gettysburg begleitete. H2 Fahnen des XXI. Korps haben ein ungewöhnliches Format im Vergleich mit denen anderer Korps; sie messen 182cm an der Stange und 121cm an der anderen Seite. H3 Nach 1863 trugen die Fahnen der meisten Kavallerie-Einheiten das traditionelle Kavalleriekorps-Abzeichen – gekreuzte Säbel. Diese Stabsfahne wurde 1864 angenommn und wurde offenbar bis zum Kriegsende getragen.